NELLIE
CASHMAN
FRONTIER ANGEL

by Robert R. O'Brien

illustrated by Daniel Clifford

Scott Foresman

Editorial Offices: Glenview, Illinois • New York, New York
Sales Offices: Reading, Massachusetts • Duluth, Georgia
Glenview, Illinois • Carrollton, Texas • Menlo Park, California

She rescued a mine owner from an angry
mob. She survived a snowslide. She hauled a
dog sled through the snow to save sick miners.
She traveled from Mexico to Alaska in search
of gold. She earned many fortunes. Then she
gave them all away to help others.

Her name was Nellie Cashman. She was a beloved woman of the Old West. She was as brave as she was pretty. She was a pioneer whose triumph over hardship changed people's ideas of what a woman could do.

If you looked at Cashman you might not guess she was so daring. She was just over five feet tall. She was thin, with large dark eyes and a pretty face. But she had a strong will and a big heart. She worked hard to make her fortune and just as hard to help others.

Cashman and her family came to America from Ireland. They left the hard times in Ireland to try to make their lives better. America was a land where people could improve themselves.

Cashman and her sister moved to San Francisco in 1869. There Cashman learned how to cook for large groups of hungry men. With that skill, she went to work in the mining camps.

After a while, she got tired of cooking. She decided to try her hand at being a prospector. And when Cashman decided to do something, she plunged right in.

She joined a gold rush to Canada in 1874. She had a long, hard trip. Once she got there, though, she made a lot of money mining for gold. She also ran a hotel for miners.

Next Cashman went south to British Columbia. A short time later, she learned that miners were sick in the camp she'd just left. She wanted to help them. She hired six men to help her bring supplies back to her sick friends. She set out in the middle of winter. The local army commander thought she was crazy. He sent soldiers to rescue her and bring her to their fort. When they found her, she was camped on the ice, brewing tea. She invited them to join her for a cup. They went back to the fort without her.

Later in the trip, Cashman set up her tent on the side of a hill. The snow was ten feet deep. It snowed all night. The next morning, one of her men went to get her. He could not find her tent. It had plunged down the hill in a snowslide. Cashman had slept through it. She dug herself out, and they went on.

Cashman made it to the mining camp. There she found that seventy-five men were very ill. She cared for all of them until they were well.

Cashman must have enjoyed excitement. Six years later she heard about silver mines in Tombstone, Arizona. Off she went. She opened a hotel in Tombstone for the miners and for travelers who came to town. The Russ Hotel was the best place in town to get a meal. Tombstone was a wild place. Miners, gamblers, and other rowdy types crowded her restaurant.

Cashman helped people who were down on their luck. The people of Tombstone loved her because she was so caring. They would never let anybody say bad things about her. One time, a stranger said he didn't like Cashman's beans. A miner who heard him stood over the man until he finished the beans.

Cashman loved the miners. But she was not afraid to tell them when they were wrong. One night she heard of a plan to threaten the owner of one of the mines. She gave the owner a ride to the train depot so he could escape. When the miners saw him riding with Cashman, they gave up their plan.

Three years later, Cashman decided to sell her hotel. She wanted to go back to mining for gold. A dying miner told her of a place in Mexico. In April of 1883, she went to Mexico with twenty other miners.

In June, a newspaper reported that Cashman had died. It said that her group of miners had run out of water. They were half right. Her party hadn't brought enough water with them.

But Nellie Cashman didn't die. She was in better shape than the rest of the group. She went for help. She trekked across the desert. She found a town with water. She didn't stop to rest. Instead, she turned around and brought water to her friends. They survived. But they all went back to Tombstone without any gold.

That trip did not stop Cashman. She still
had dreams of mining. She went to mining
camps all over the West. Sometimes she mined
for gold. Sometimes she mined for silver. Some
people say she even went to South Africa to
look for diamonds.

In 1898, Nellie Cashman joined the great
Klondike gold rush. She went to Alaska. She
camped on the edge of Lake Laberge. She
waited out the bitter winter. When the ice
melted, she built a boat. With a feeling of
triumph, she rode the rapids on the Yukon
River and went to Dawson City.

In Dawson City, Cashman opened a restaurant and store. She helped out many a poor and hungry miner. Her store was called "The Haven of Rest." The miners had so much respect for her that each time she came into a dining room or dance hall, they would stand.

Cashman also had very good luck with mining. She went all over Alaska and Canada by snowshoe and dogsled. She found one spot that earned her over $100,000. But most of that money went to helping others or buying new mines.

Cashman spent the rest of her life busily traveling all over the North. She even went to the edge of the Arctic Circle. When she was in her seventies, she got a sled-dog team. They traveled 750 miles across Alaska. Wherever she went, she looked for a fortune to find and friends to help. She didn't keep her fortunes. But she did keep her many friends—all the way to the end of her days.